Mother

PATIENCE STRONG

Frederick Muller Ltd
London

Those Wonderful Years

It all went too quickly the fun and the laughter — the wild days, the child days — for Life followed after and brought its own burdens to lay on my back — but sometimes when things looked their worst, bleak and black — I often remembered and laughed in my mind — at something those wonderful years left behind.

Something That Belonged to Mother

Often when I'm looking for a thing I have
mislaid — I come on some forgotten odds and
ends. Time seems to fade — and in a flash
leap across the years because I see — things
that stab my heart awake with Mother's
memory.

A photograph, some beads, a thimble — kept I
know not why — a sentimental whim has
always made me put them by — and so they
keep on turning up to haunt me through the
years — It's foolish, but I cling to them —
these little souvenirs.

The Blessing

The blessing of a loving mother nobody
can measure — You cannot put it into
words or price this precious
treasure . . . She suffers when you suffer
and she shares in your success. She
works for you and wishes for your
health and happiness.

Your love express in words before she
passes on her way — then there'll be no
sadness over what you failed to say . . . It
is now that kindness counts; we
sometimes leave too late — a thank you
for some little thing that we appreciate.

The Centre of the Home

Mother makes the home; she is the centre of it all — on duty day and night, at everybody's beck and call ... loving, serving, giving, she's the one who understands. The family is held together by one pair of hands. One day, someday, those same hands may need another's care — another's strength to lean upon, another's home to share.

Mother Nature

In spite of all the wars and feuds within the world
to-day — the work of Nature still goes on ... Spring
dances on her way; she laughs at our disturbances,
our terrors and alarms, with sunlight gleaming in her
hair and blossoms in her arms.

In spite of man with all his might, his folly and his
sin — the gentle voice of Mother Nature sounds above
the din . . . Above the turmoil and the roar we hear the
beat of wings — the stirring in the budding hedge of
furred and feathered things.

To Thank You

How can I say it? How can I make you
understand that I — appreciated all
you did as year by year went by? You
helped and you encouraged me in all I
tried to do — but perhaps the greatest
debt is what I owe to you — in giving
me a faith to follow and a golden rule
— the lovely things, the holy things that
are not taught in school.

You gave me my first Bible and you
taught me how to read it. No doubt you,
knew that life was tough and how much
I should need it — how in times of
trouble to this treasure I would cling.
Thank you, mother, thank you dear, for
this — and everything.

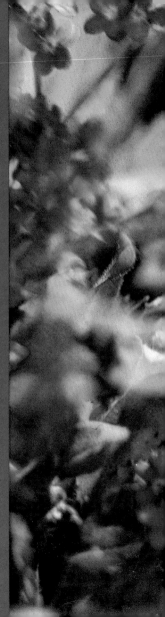

Forget Me Not

Forget-me-not. Your dainty sky-blue
flowerlets seem to bring — fragrant
recollections of beloved names that
cling — around the heart; sweet
memories of dear souls who have gone:
Mother, brother, husband, sister,
friend . . . but Love lives on.

Voices from the world of spirit breathe
through memory — whispering of past
delights and of the joys to be — turning
thought from earthly things and from
our human lot. Far away their voices
seem to say — Forget me not.

Come Back Soon

We miss you more than we can say — every
hour of every day: the mainstay of the family
— so make a quick recovery.

Home's not home if you're not there — the
vacant place, the empty chair . . . We're all
upset and out of tune — just muddling on.
Please come back soon.

Always Young

I'm always young while you are here.
You are my childhood, mother dear.
You are my youth. Your smiling face —
comes haunting every secret place —
within the caves of memory — for you
were always there with me — in all
those wonderful events — of the years
of innocence — when the sun shone
every day — Or so it seemed; all fun
and play — Life was one long lovely
Spring — There was a bloom on
everything.

While you're still near I catch the glow
— reflected from the long ago. Stay,
dear Mother, Never go.

The Comforter

When memories go wandering along life's
winding track — step by step they always seem
at last to lead us back — to Mother and the
recollections of those early years. She it was
who healed our hurts and kissed away our
tears . . . Mother was the comforter Her touch
with reassure. In her arms a little frightened
soul would feel secure.

The Christmas Mother

A Hebrew girl betrothed to Joseph, pure and
undefiled — was chosen by God to be the
mother of the Holy Child — sent to Israel, the
Saviour of the human race. Mary knew it as
she bore him in that humble place . . . For
Gabriel at Nazareth had told her of these
things — how she would become the mother of
the King of Kings.

Meekly did she acquiesce and noised it not
abroad — accepting with the words, Behold,
the handmaid of the Lord! . . . Spirit of
humility, obedient and good — glorifying for
all time the role of Motherhood.

If You Can Remember

It's something to be thankful for — if
you can remember — a Mother who
was good and wise and kind ... It's
something to be grateful for if in Life's
November — you can look back on the
past and find — a Mother who was
always at the door. Could a child expect
or wish for more? A simple home where
Love made its abode — a haven at the
end of every road.

Mother of the Bride

She has played her part and now there's
nothing to be done — but play the charming
hostess with a smile for everyone...There she
is, a radiant figure, elegant and smart —
although we know just how she must be feeling
in her heart.

For her, as well as for her girl, it is the day of
days. She knows it is a milestone and the ending
of a phase — but ends are new beginnings
where the roads of life divide. So Time be kind
— and may God bless the Mother of the bride.

The Best Friend of All

Mother cannot drop her burden. She goes
plodding on — even when she's weary and her
strength is all but gone . . . Mother just goes on
though life at times is hard to bear. Mother
goes on being Mother. Mother must be there
— to do what things are needed for on her so
much depends: the faithful one, the loving
one, the best of all our friends.

The Secret Cord

Many sisters I may have and more than
one dear brother — Many friends I've
made but I have only got one
Mother . . . No tie could be as strong as
that which holds between us two — no
bond could be as close. You're part of
me, I'm part of you . . . It is understood.
No word is said — none need be spoken
— the cord that links our lives together
never can be broken.

For Memory's Sake

Many things we do for memory's sake — Along
forgotten paths long journeys make — to keep alive
the thought of one once dear — with whom we shared
the best from year to year . . . We can't explain nor can
we understand — how we are guided by an unseen
hand — to follow where the heart directs and make —
a gesture to the past — for memory's sake.